PLANES
OF THE ISLE of MAN
1945 ~ present day

BARRY EDWARDS

Published on the Isle of Man by
Lily Publications, PO Box 33, Ramsey, Isle of Man IM99 4LP
Tel: +44 (0)1624 898446   Fax: +44 (0)1624 898449
E-mail: info@lilypublications.co.uk   Web: www.lilypublications.co.uk

INTRODUCTION

This is the final volume in a series of eight books based around the vast Manx transport photograph collection of Stan Basnett. The series has covered all aspects of transport both on and around the Island.

The very first flight from the Isle of Man was on Monday 10th November 1902, when two balloonists took off from Peveril Square, adjacent to the Sea Terminal, and flew up past Maughold Head and on to Dumfries, travelling the 77 miles in just four and a half hours.

The Island will celebrate the centenary of powered flight from Manx soil on 4th July 2011. On that day nearly a century ago, a small biplane took off from Nobles Park to the delight of the many spectators assembled to witness the event.

Blackpool and West Coast Air Services operated the first commercial flights in 1933 with a daily service between the Island and Blackpool. Soon Liverpool was added and gradual expansion occurred over a number of years.

The story told in this book begins 12 years after these first commercial flights and just at the end of the Second World War when air travel was beginning to get back on its feet.

Isle of Man Air Services had maintained regular services throughout the war years but the nationalisation of all such airlines was begun in February 1947 and completed on 1st August that year. British European Airways Corporation now had control of all internal flights. The demise of Isle of Man Air Services was disappointing for the Island, the company making Ronaldsway the second busiest airport after Croydon in pre-war days.

Air racing returned to the skies of the Island in 1947 and it was not long before smaller companies began to emerge to give BEA some competition. Manx Charter Experts was soon renamed Manx Air Charters Ltd and in early 1948 Mannin Airways appeared on the scene. Towards the end of the 1940s North West Airlines (IOM) Ltd was formed by Mannin Airways and Ulster Aviation, to fill gaps caused by the withdrawal of BEA from several Island services.

Maybe this was to set the aviation scene for the Island for many years to come, as even today the routes and operators are far from stable.

The Manx Airlines name first appeared in 1953, lasting the first time until 1957 when it was absorbed into the Silver City operation. It was not then until 1982 when Terry Liddiard, then employed by British Midland became Director and General Manager of the new Manx Airlines under an agreement between British Midland and Air UK.

Manx Airlines provided the longest period of stability for the ever increasing numbers of passengers travelling to and from the Island. The new airline went from strength to strength, beginning life with just four leased in aircraft and ending up with a fleet of over 50, when it suffered a similar fate to that of its earlier namesake. It became part of British Airways CitiExpress in March 2002, that franchise changing its name to BA Connect just a couple of years later. Continuing problems led to the eventual 'purchase' of BA Connect by Flybe.

As the Manx Airlines takeover was under way a new company EuroManx, originally owned by Belfast-based Woodgate Aviation appeared and started with routes to Dublin and Edinburgh. This airline survived for just less than six years, the last flights operating on 8th May 2007. Meanwhile another organisation, initially a fledgling of Blue Island based on Guernsey began operating to Blackpool and Belfast. Manx2.com soon expanded and have introduced some interesting and successful destinations such as Gloucester and more recently, a few services to Anglesey.

An enthusiast visiting Ronaldsway today will find Aer Arann, Blue Island, Easyjet, Flybe and Manx2.com aircraft.

DE HAVILLAND RAPIDES

Manx Air Charters Ltd,
De Havilland 89 Rapide
G-AJGV Glen Wyllin and
89A Rapide G-AKGY Glen
Maye, outside their hangar
at Ronaldsway.

(Terry Faragher Collection)

The Island has two other workable airstrips, both in the north at Andreas and Jurby. An earlier grass strip at Hall Caine has long since disappeared. There are also a couple of short private grass landing strips and a number of helicopter landing places dotted around the Island.

Andreas is now privately owned and operational although without a formal control tower. A number of private aircraft are based at the airfield and at certain times it becomes busy with visiting light aircraft, in particular during the annual TT Festival and Manx Grand Prix fortnight.

Just a few miles to the west is Jurby, once RAF Jurby. Sadly despite recent superb air shows, this airfield sees little activity except from the local model aircraft flyers who make good use of the available space. Parts of the runway although technically still available for flying, are used as a race track for both motorcycle and car events. One aircraft that does still reside at Jurby tucked away in a hangar is Leopard Moth G-ACLL.

Manx Flyers have a super base at Ronaldsway and the Manx Aviation Museum is situated adjacent to the taxiway between the terminal buildings and 08 threshold, providing superb views of departing aircraft. The introduction of the Manx Register in 2007 had allowed local and indeed many aircraft from far afield to carry the 'M' prefix.

Despite the uncertainty over who will be operating flights in the future, the Island provides a very wide variety of aircraft types for the enthusiast, and plenty of good places from which to watch and photograph the many aircraft coming and going.

It is now some three years since Miles Cowsill of Lily Publications and Stan approached me about authoring this volume. It has given me great pleasure to sort through the literally hundreds of pictures available to me for the book. Sincere thanks are due to David Ashworth, Stan Basnett, Richard Davis, Terry Faragher, Martin Nelson, Philip Pain and Jon Wornham for making their collections available for inclusion. My thanks go once again to Miles and Linda Cowsill at Lily Publications and to my wife Irene for her patience while many hours are spent in front of the computer.

Barry Edwards
Ballasalla
Isle of Man
December 2010

An unidentified Vickers 491 Viking of the King's Flight arrives at Ronaldsway with the Duke of Edinburgh on Senior Race Day in June 1947. This will be one of six of this type, available to the King's Flight at this time.

(Terry Faragher Collection)

G-AIHZ (c/n 6905) Miles Hawk/Beech Aircraft Corporation BEECH D17S outside one of the Jurby hangars during the 1947 Isle of Man Air Races. *(Terry Faragher Collection)*

Auster J1 Autocrat, thought to be G-AGXN (c/n 1963), at Jurby Airfield while on static display for the Isle of Man Air Races on 24th to 28th May 1947.

(Terry Faragher Collection)

British European Airways Av Roe and Co Ltd Avro C19 Series 1 G-AHID (c/n 1319). Inherited from Railway Air Services in 1947 it was transferred to the Ministry of Civil Aviation for re-sale in 1948.

(Terry Faragher Collection)

British European Airways Douglas Aircraft Company Inc Douglas C47 Dakota 3 and Av Roe and Co Ltd Avro C19 Series 1 G-AGIU 'Pionair' Edward Busk and G-AHIG (c/n 12096 and c/n 1322) at Liverpool Speke airport, captured by the camera in late 1947. *(Terry Faragher Collection)*

Island based North West Airlines provided this Miles M57 Aerovan 4 G-AJKU (c/n 6407) to bring milk to the Island during the milk shortage of 1949. Built at Newtownards in Northern Ireland the aircraft was with North West from May 1951 until April 1954 when it was permanently withdrawn from use. *(Terry Faragher Collection)*

Av Roe and Co Ltd 652A Anson 1 G-AIRN (c/n NK667) was captured by the camera while on lease to Starways in May 1949. The aircraft was later purchased and sold on again in February 1952. It was withdrawn from service on 28th July 1952. *(Terry Faragher Collection)*

De Havilland Aircraft Co Ltd DH82A Tiger Moth G-AKXC (c/n N6776) while owned by Mannin Airways Ltd, Isle of Man as shown on the front of the fuselage. The aircraft was built in 1939 and was with Mannin from 18th August 1948 until 2nd July 1949. It was powered by a single De Havilland Gipsy Major 1 engine. *(Terry Faragher Collection)*

Two similar DH89A Rapides sit beside the Ronaldsway control tower in 1950. Nearest the camera is G-AHGH (c/n 6934) built by Brush Coachworks Ltd in 1946 and G-AFEZ (c/n 6408) built eight years earlier by the De Havilland Aircraft Co Ltd in 1938. Of interest is the large '09' sign on the front of the control tower, an indication to pilots that runway 09 is in use. *(Terry Faragher Collection)*

A rare visit by a British European Airways King Arthur Class Bristol 171 Sycamore helicopter to Ronaldsway in the 1950s. BEA owned two of the type and for a while had a third on loan from Bristol. Sadly the aircraft is unidentified. *(Terry Faragher Collection)*

One of several official postcards produced for BKS Air Transport Ltd, with Douglas Aircraft Company Inc Douglas C47 Dakota 3s. The aircrafts G-AMSH and G-AMVB (c/n 16583 and c/n 14637) are captured by the official camera, during an air-to-air shoot over the Island in the early 1950s.

(Terry Faragher Collection)

Douglas Aircraft Company Inc C47A Dakota 3 G-AGHF (c/n 9186) operated by North West Airlines (Isle of Man) Ltd is captured by the camera during routine maintenance at Croydon Airport in 1950. North West was formed in 1948 by Mannin Airways Ltd and Ulster Aviation Ltd.
(Terry Faragher Collection)

Air Lingus DC3 EI-ACH (c/n 12896) 'Columban' during a visit to Ronaldsway, alongside another DC3 of British European Airways. The aircraft are in front of the old tower at Ronaldsway. *(Terry Faragher Collection)*

Bristol Aeroplane Co Ltd Bristol B170 Mk.21 Wayfarer G-AIFM (c/n 12773) *City of Carlisle* at Ronaldsway. This aircraft had two operating stints with Silver City, the first from December 1951 until March 1954, the second from October 1957 until February 1965 when it was withdrawn from service.
(Terry Faragher Collection)

Douglas C47B Dakota 3 G-ANAE (c/n 26101/43-48840), formerly RAF KJ930, built in 1943, entered service with Lancashire Aircraft Corporation in June 1953 and is seen here loading passengers at Ronaldsway during the summer of the same year.
(Terry Faragher Collection)

Helicopter Services Ltd operated this Costruzioni Aeronautiche Giovanni Agusta, Agusta Bell 47G-1 Helicopter G-AODJ (c/n 044) for eight years from September 1955. It visited Ronaldsway in 1956 and was captured by the camera during re-fuelling.

(*Terry Faragher Collection*)

Silver City Airways De Havilland Aircraft Co Ltd DH90A Dragonfly G-AEWZ (c/n 7555) is seen outside the Manx Airlines hangar at Ronaldsway following completion of its Certificate of Airworthiness overhaul. (*Terry Faragher Collection*)

Manx Airlines engineers A. Simpson, K. Dyke, J. Kelly and T. Watterson carry out pre-flight checks to Douglas Aircraft Company Inc Douglas C47B Dakota 4 G-AMZC (c/n 16522) in front of the main terminal building at Ronaldsway. Sadly, on the morning of Thursday 22nd December 1955, while positioning in preparation for a charter flight this aircraft crashed on approach to Dusseldorf airport with the loss of three lives. (*Terry Faragher Collection*)

Scottish Aviation Ltd Twin Pioneer 3 G-AOEO (c/n 503) is lined up awaiting take-off from an unidentified location. The aircraft made at least one visit to the Island during its very short life. Constructed in 1955 at Prestwick, it was lost in an incident near Tripoli in December 1957 *(Terry Faragher Collection)*

Douglas DC3 Dakota G-APML (c/n 14175/25620) taxies out towards the runway at a somewhat different looking Ronaldsway. The large dark coloured hangar, known as hangar 1, has recently been demolished while the two Nissen style sheds showing the wording 'Cambrian' are still in existence but have the two large hangars built during the reign of Manx Airlines just beyond them. *(Richard Davis)*

A regular visitor to Ronaldsway from 1955 to 1958 was this Percival Aircraft Co Ltd P50 Prince 4 G-AMLY (c/n P50-45). It was owned by Martin Baker Aircraft Co Ltd and was used to transport ejector seat parts to and from their Island facility, conveniently situated just across the road from the airport. *(Terry Faragher Collection)*

De Havilland Aircraft Co Ltd, 114 Heron 1B G-AOZN (c/n 14005). This aircraft was leased to Manx Airlines from Silver City Airways in 1957 and 1958. The aircraft carries the original Manx Airlines roundel on the tail. *(Terry Faragher Collection)*

Cambrian Viscount displaying Viscount Jet Prop on the fuselage side, captured shortly after arriving on stand at Ronaldsway on 10th April 1963. The propellers are still rotating and no ground staff have arrived, so it will be a few minutes before the passengers are allowed to disembark. The aircraft G-AMON (c/n 27) first flew in January 1954 and was broken up at Southend in 1979. *(Stan Basnett)*

A close-up of the forward fuselage of G-APML shows the detail of these fine aircraft and the Pratt & Whitney R-1830-90D engine and its three-bladed propeller. In the background can be seen Viscount G-AOYI. *(Richard Davis)*

Bristol Aeroplane Co Ltd, Bristol 170 Mk.11a G-AIME (c/n 12795) is seen getting airborne from Ronaldsway during October 1962. The aircraft is in the livery of Silver City Airways for whom it flew between 1950 and 1956, returning in 1957. It was named City of Exeter in 1959 before the company changed its name to British United Air Ferries in 1963, and it was withdrawn in October 1963, finally being broken up at Southend in May 1964. (Stan Basnett)

In the days when security was not such an issue at our airports, the photographer was able to get this view of Beagle Aircraft Limited, Beagle A109 G-ASCB (c/n B527) as it taxied off the runway after landing on 10th April 1963. Interestingly the aircraft appears to be only partly painted. (Stan Basnett)

A super picture taken from about where Viscount House now stands, shows Dakota C47 G-AMWV (c/n 25600) in full British United Colours with Vickers Viscount G-AMON (c/n 27) in Cambrian Livery behind on 18th April 1963. The departure lounge and arrivals areas now extend behind the Viscount and the control tower's days are numbered following the completion of a new tower that sits about behind the tail of the Viscount. (Stan Basnett)

The Ronaldsway control tower is shown with its roof mounted Radar, since removed, as Dart Herald G-APWJ (c/n 158), displaying the livery of British United Airlines is prepared for its next flight on 3rd June 1966. This aircraft was eventually donated to the Duxford Aviation Society where it has been restored and is now on public display.
(Stan Basnett)

During the May 1965 Manx Air Rally, Jurby airfield plays host to DH84 Dragon 2 G-ADDI (c/n 6096) in the bright livery of Chrisair. This nine seater biplane began life with Railway Air Services in March 1935 and is still in flying condition in America and registered N34DH. *(Stan Basnett)*

Taking part in the May 1965 Manx Air Rally was this Jodel DR105A G-ASAB (c/n 87), captured by the camera as it flew over Jurby Airfield. The very square wings are somewhat unusual. *(Stan Basnett)*

Queen's Flight Hawker Siddeley HS-748 Andover CC2 (Srs2/206) XS789 (c/n 1561) on the tarmac at Ronaldsway in June 1969. The passenger departure lounge now occupies the area where the aircraft is parked, the control tower now closed and replaced. Another aircraft is just visible above the hangars on its approach to runway 27, now 26. *(Stan Basnett)*

RAF De Havilland Devon VP963 (c/n 04213) on a visit to Ronaldsway in January 1970. The area behind the aircraft was known as the 'torpedo section' and the tall building immediately behind the aircraft was the torpedo attack training area. *(Stan Basnett)*

On 27th January 1970 Hawker Siddeley Andover XS596 (c/n 1574) is on the west apron at Ronaldsway in an impressive camouflage livery. More recently based at Boscombe Down it was known as the 'UK open skies aircraft' and was latterly operated in this role by Qinetiq. The similarity to both the HS748 and the later ATP is clear, indeed the Andover production numbers are in the 748 sequence. *(Stan Basnett)*

This bright liveried De Havilland DH104 Dove aircraft G-ANOV (c/n 04445) began life with the then Ministry of Transport and Civil Aviation in March 1954 and remained with the organisation right through until its withdrawal by the Civil Aviation Authority in July 1981. It is now preserved at the Museum of Flight near Edinburgh. It is seen here whilst on a visit to Ronaldsway in January 1970, and is captured while taxiing on the main 09/27 now 08/26 runway. *(Stan Basnett)*

Westland Wessex helicopters from RAF Valley with XT681 (c/n WA549) nearest the camera, the machine behind remains unidentified, on the tarmac at Ronaldsway during February 1970. The presence of the fuel truck would indicate the reason for the visit. (*Stan Basnett*)

A very rare visit by an unidentified US Air Force Convair B29 seen here landing on what was then runway 04/22 now 03/21 during February 1970. The aircraft was bringing US officials to the Island following the crash of a Super Sabre over the Irish Sea bombing range. (*Stan Basnett*)

A super close-up of a Westland Wessex helicopter XT681 (c/n WA549) from RAF Valley in flight, passing between the control tower and the main terminal building! 3rd February 1970. *(Stan Basnett)*

A major resurface of the main runway at Ronaldsway appears to be underway, and despite the fact that not one of the workers would admit to being a plane spotter, all eyes are on the sky above as an unidentified BAC1-11 produces a trail of exhaust while practising ILS approaches on 14th February 1970. Certainly, some fair quantities of tar need laying before anything will be able to land. *(Stan Basnett)*

The BAC1-11 was an impressive looking creature as shown in this super March 1970 view of Cambrian G-AVOE (c/n 129) while on stand at Ronaldsway. The 1-11s were to have a long career with the Island, the type seeing service with Manx Airlines and the author recalls a flight back to London in a leased 1-11 in the late 1980s. Manx used another example as late as the mid 1990s. *(Stan Basnett)*

On 7th March 1970 Ronaldsway was covered in snow, as an unidentified Vickers Viscount prepares to take off, its propellers throwing back a cloud of snow in their thrust. The runway is shortened by the use of temporary barriers and the workmen have obviously gone home for the day, leaving their wheelbarrow out in the cold. The incomplete 09/27 runway was in use due to severe crosswinds preventing the use of the shorter 04/22 runway. King William's College is visible behind the aircraft. *(Stan Basnett)*

Douglas DC6B OO-CTN (c/n 44176) in the livery of Sabena makes a fine sight parked on the apron at Ronaldsway during August 1970. It appears that this picture was taken during some form of event as it would not be normal practice to be able to park your car alongside the tarmac. (Stan Basnett)

Reims Aviation Sa Cessna FR172F Reims Rocket, G-AWWU (c/n 0111), taking part in the June 1970 Air Rally over Jurby. This aircraft is still flying from its home in the west of England. (Stan Basnett)

RAF Handley Page HP-67 Hastings T5 TG511 (c/n 511), on west hard standing at Ronaldsway on 3rd June 1970. This fine looking aircraft is now preserved as part of the cold war collection at the RAF Museum, Cosford. (Stan Basnett)

An unidentified Andover of the Queen's Flight arrives at Ronaldsway on 25th June 1971 with the British Prime Minister on board, visiting the Island to attend a NALGO conference. The fenced area visible under the aircraft is part of the meteorological office weather station. *(Stan Basnett)*

An impressive looking beast arriving at Ronaldsway with its load of horses. It is an Armstrong Whitworth Aircraft Ltd AW650 ARGOSY 101, registered G-AZHN (c/n 6657) and is seen taxiing up to the apron area on a misty August day in 1973. *(Stan Basnett)*

De Havilland DH104 Dove G-ASPA (c/n 04536) awaits its next passengers in the Ronaldsway sunshine during August 1973. It is interesting to note that it is possible to see straight through the aircraft, the far wing visible through the second window. *(Stan Basnett)*

The Armstrong Whitworth Argossy G-AZHN (c/n 6657) again, showing one of the horses being unloaded.

(Stan Basnett)

A super view of IOM Flying Centre Reims Aviation Sa Cessna F172H Skyhawk, G-AWMZ (c/n 0554) on the ground at Ronaldsway. The aircraft first flew in August 1968 and was withdrawn in September 1981.

(Stan Basnett)

Over the years the Jurby Day air shows have produced some rare visitors to the Island's air space. Preserved with a British Registration G-BEDF (c/n 8693) is former US Air Force Boeing Airplane Co B-17G Flying Fortress (44-85784), over the airfield during August 1980. *(Stan Basnett)*

This Air Commuter PA31 Navajo Chieftain G-BAVM (c/n 31-7305029) appears to be sheltering under the wing of a much larger aircraft as it enjoys a rest between duties on the Island. The visibility from these small but popular aircraft is superb through the large windows and the lack of bulkhead behind the pilot allowing a good view forward. *(David Ashworth)*

Many organisations try to use aircraft registrations that reflect their company initials. Such is the case with this Hawker Siddeley HS125/700B G-CCAA (c/n 257130) in service with the Civil Aviation Authority. During a brief visit to the Island the aircraft is seen parked just below the control tower and in front of the old wooden pier. *(David Ashworth)*

Morris Motors Ltd DH82A Tiger Moth G-AYIT (c/n 86343) climbs steeply while entertaining the crowds below at the 1981 Jurby air show. The aircraft was transferred to the Brazilian register in March 2007. *(Stan Basnett)*

When BEA ceased operations in 1974 and merged with the British Overseas Airways Corporation to form British Airways, a number of its aircraft were fully repainted into British Airways livery. One example was this Viscount 806 G-AOYL (c/n 261) seen here on approach to Ronaldsway. The aircraft went on to serve British Air Ferries and British World Airlines and was finally broken up at Southend in February 1993. *(Stan Basnett)*

Probably one of the best known wartime aircraft is the Avro Lancaster Bomber. Seen here flying over Jurby as part of the 1981 air show is an unidentified machine against a clear blue sky on 16th August. *(Stan Basnett)*

RAF Nimrods make regular visits to the Island on practice flights, usually for approach training at Ronaldsway. On this occasion XV240 (c/n 8015) is making itself heard over Jurby on 16th August 1981 as part of the display sequence for that year's air show. *(Stan Basnett)*

A type that is no stranger to the Island is the RAF Hercules Transport plane. This type C-1K XV201 (c/n 4227) brings the Falcon Parachute display team over Jurby on 16th August 1981. On at least one occasion the author recalls one of the type bringing the daily papers, on a particularly windy day, when even the daily ferry was cancelled. *(Stan Basnett)*

The very first Manx Airlines flight was operated by this Embraer E110 Banderantie G-RLAY (c/n 110364). The aircraft remained in Genair colours but had Manx markings and titling. Captured by the camera, it is seen here at Ronaldsway with a Manx labelled ground power unit attached. The GPU is used to provide the electrical power used to start the engines and will be disconnected once the start has been completed. (David Ashworth)

Kilroe Helicopters' Augusta Bell 206B Jetranger 2 G-TKHM (c/n 8557) demonstrates its air ambulance capabilities in conjunction with City Air Links' PA31-350 Navajo Chieftain. The demonstration took place at the Jurby air show on 15th August 1982 and the scenario consisted of a patient being ferried in from an inaccessible part of the IOM for onward transfer in G-CITY in Air Ambulance configuration. Note both the rear passenger and freight doors are open thus making the Chieftain's cabin accessible to a patient on a stretcher. (David Ashworth)

Fokker F27s were also once regular visitors but visits are now rare. Displaying full Air UK livery G-BDVS (c/n 10232) is captured at an unidentified location between duties. The aircraft was eventually put into store at Norwich in September 1994 and broken up in December 1996. *(Author's Collection)*

Handley Page Dart Herald 214 G-BEBB (c/n 186) is captured at Ronaldsway in the bright and bold Chanel Express livery. The wooden pier buildings seen in the background were replaced by the existing departure lounge in the mid 1990s and the control tower is still in use, albeit a replacement is under construction.

(David Ashworth)

Dan-Air operated a wide range of flights from the Island, often using their fleet of HS748s. Just getting off stand and about to begin its taxi to the runway is full liveried G-AXVG (c/n 1589). Ronaldsway has seen just about every Hawker Siddeley/BAe/Avro civilian type over the years, ATPs and J31s are still almost daily visitors. *(David Ashworth)*

A spectacular visitor to Jurby air show was this Lockheed C141A Starlifter 438/67-0022 (c/n 300-6273). It appeared spot on time for its display slot despite having flown direct from the USA, a flight that had taken around nine hours. *(David Ashworth)*

The Island is well used to boats and planes but, this must be the ultimate! Making a very rare visit is Consolidated Aircraft PBY-5A Catalina flying boat G-BLSC (c/n 1997) over Ronaldsway during September 1985. *(Stan Basnett)*

The agility of a helicopter is demonstrated here by this Augusta Bell 206B Jetranger 2, that has landed on the sloping ground adjacent to the former Majestic Hotel in Onchan. Operated by East Coast Helicopters it is registered G-BKDA (c/n 8337). The aircraft is obviously staying a while as the rotor blades have been tied down to prevent wind damage. *(David Ashworth)*

A fine study of Manx Airlines Shorts SD360 G-WACK (c/n 3611) resting between duties at Ronaldsway, with 146/100 G-OJET in the background. One has to hope that the aircraft did not live up to its registration at any time during its operating life! *(David Ashworth)*

Flying over the city of Liverpool on approach to Liverpool John Lennon, formerly Speke, airport is Manx Airlines Saab 340 G-HOPP (c/n 008) with Sky Hopper markings. The aircraft was usually used on the Liverpool to Heathrow route but did make regular visits to the Island. *(Author's Collection)*

A one time regular at Ronaldsway was this privately owned Beech Aircraft Corporation, Beech 300LW, popularly known as a Super Kingair G-SRES (c/n FA39). It was photographed during an overnight stop on the east apron, while being looked after by the photographer. (*David Ashworth*)

On 30th November 1987 Manx Airlines took delivery of their first 146 jet in the form of 146/100 G-OJET. Very much welcomed by the residents of Castletown for its quiet take-off, this aircraft made history on 4th December, when it became the first 146 to operate into London Heathrow on a passenger service. 146s operated daily to Heathrow up to and including the very last flight, with 146/200 G-MIMA on 30th March 2002. (*David Ashworth*)

This Shorts SD360 G-OLGW (c/n 3741) is in Leeds/Bradford based Capital livery. Capital provided some cargo services to the Island in the late 1980s. The aircraft later joined the Titan Airways fleet as G-ZAPD and was still flying as late as 2009 in America as N875RR. (*Author's Collection*)

Vickers Viscount 836 G-BFZL (c/n 836) wearing temporary Manx Airlines markings while on short term lease to the company and captured by the camera on 12th April 1990. BFZL had been their last Viscount in regular service but, is seen here making one of several 'encores' in service with them. (*Philip Pain*)

Jurby airfield in the north of the Island is just about the windiest place possible for an airfield. Here we have DH82A Tiger Moth G-AGYU (c/n 85265) taxiing past the short lived airship hangar. After a particularly wild night, what remained of the hangar was strewn all over Jurby, its concrete base is now used as a go-kart track, while the aircraft survives in flying condition. (*Jon Wornham*)

Another airline that has had a long association with the Island is Flybe. In its early days it was known as Spacegrand, later becoming Jersey European, then British European before adopting its current name. In 1990 Jersey European were operating this Fokker F27 9Q-CBD (c/n 10687) seen here about to take off from Jersey airport. (*David Ashworth*)

During the early 1990s the Advanced Airship Corporation began construction of an advanced non-rigid airship in a purpose built hangar at Jurby airfield. The first airship designated ANR-1 was never actually completed and no others were started. The first was allocated registration G-MAAC (c/n 01). These two parts, one of the main fins and rudder, are all that is known to survive of G-MAAC, currently stored in a nearby hangar but, surely worthy of preservation. (*Barry Edwards*)

Jersey European had a number of F27s in their fleet and were usually to be found on the Bristol service in later years. Here F27/500 G-JEAA (c/n 10664) is seen taxiing towards its parking stand. (*Author's Collection*)

There can be few airports that can claim to have seen every member of a particular type on its tarmac. Over the years Ronaldsway must have had a visit from just about every ATP. First operated by Manx Airlines, later British Airways, who operated 17 of the 65 finished aircraft, they appeared for Emerald Airways and more recently Atlantic and West Air who have now merged to become West Atlantic with a full ATP maintenance facility on the Island. Here we see G-BUUP (c/n 2008) later G-MANU at Liverpool. (*Author's Collection*)

There is something awesome about the Hercules aircraft. Capable of flying even in the worst conditions, the type has seen service all over the world. Taking part in the 1982 Jurby Air show is US Air Force C130 rescue Hercules 5820. A second Hercules can be seen in the background. *(David Ashworth)*

Australian-registered aircraft are not regular visitors to Ronaldsway, so the arrival of this Aero Commander of Aerodata VH-MEH (c/n 3258) on 3rd June 1992, caused some excitement among the resident enthusiasts. The aircraft has a modified tail with large survey probe attached. *(Philip Pain)*

Fokker 100 of TAT European Airlines F-GIOF (c/n 11363), photographed on 15th June 1992. Arriving with a demonstration flight by the manufacturer for the benefit of Manx Airlines Europe, who at that time were expanding their fleet and looking at various regional jet types. *(Philip Pain)*

Army Westland SA-341B Gazelle AH1 ZA771 (c/n WA1813) of 654 Squadron visited Jurby on 21st July 1992 during exercise 'Double Eagle'. As far as it is known, this was the only aircraft ever to appear on the Island, still in its 'Gulf War' colours. *(Philip Pain)*

Boeing 737-236 G-BGDS (c/n 21806) of GB Airways, named 'Mons Calpe', visited Ronaldsway on 24th April 1993. The aircraft was operating an inclusive charter flight and making a rare visit by this airline. *(Philip Pain)*

Hawker Siddley 748 Andover E.3A XS644 (c/n Set28) of 32 Squadron based at RAF Northolt is seen at Ronaldsway on 30th April 1993. The aircraft had brought in a military band and was one of only a couple of the type to receive the low-visibility grey colour scheme. *(Philip Pain)*

Percival Q6 G-AFFD (c/n Q21), one of only 26 built, is the second aircraft completed in 1938 for Sir Phillip Sassoon, shown here in the Aeroservices (IOM) hangar on 9th May 1993. This was about as far advanced as the on-Island restoration of this unique survivor proceeded. The unfinished project was sold to a restorer in England in 2007, and it finally left the Island by road in late 2008. *(Philip Pain)*

A demonstrator at Ronaldsway. This Canadair CRJ100ER C-GVRJ (c/n 7003) taxies onto stand 2 to be shown off by the management of Manx Airlines, who at the time were trying to decide on what type of regional jet should be purchased. Sadly the efforts of Bombardier were without rewards as the company chose the Embraer 145 instead. *(Jon Wornham)*

BAe ATP G-BUUR (c/n 2024) in the livery of LAR Portugal, for whom it had operated as CS-TGC, is seen on 12th July 1993. It had just returned to the Manx Airlines Engineering base at the end of the lease agreement. *(Philip Pain)*

Boeing 757-200 G-IEAB (c/n 24636) of Inter European Airways at Ronaldsway on an IT charter, on 3rd September 1993. This was the first ever visit of a 757, and the (then) largest ever aircraft to use the airport. A series of photographs were taken for future airport publicity purposes, only to be spoilt when Inter European ceased to exist shortly afterwards. *(Philip Pain)*

BAC One-Eleven 479 ZE432 (c/n 250) of the Empire Test Pilots School based at Boscombe Down, at Ronaldsway on 28th September 1993, prior to departure with local Air Cadets for a weekend visit to Boscombe. There were no landing charges raised for any military flights that came in to pick up Air Cadets, this meant that if any military aircraft were on a training flight, it could collect the Cadets at no additional cost. This, and the return flight, were the only ever visits by a military One-Eleven. *(Philip Pain)*

P126 Lockheed Jetstar N500NM (c/n 2368) belonging to Nigel Mansell, photographed on 18th April 1994, when he came to open the new departure lounge. Other than his very occasional visits in this aircraft, it was a very rare type of early transatlantic executive jet for the Island. *(Philip Pain)*

BAe Jetstream 3109 G-BTAI (c/n 758) prior to delivery to Cassovia Air, Czechoslovakia, was seen at Ronaldsway on 20th April 1994. It was to become OM-SKY but, was operating some scheduled flights for Manx Airlines who were using Jetstream 31 aircraft on their new Cardiff services. (Philip Pain)

During their lifetime many aircraft receive several repaints and often several changes of livery. One such machine is Jetstream 41 G-MAJA (c/n 41032) that is now flying for Eastern Airways. It began life painted in British Midland colours and has been through Manx Airlines old, Manx Airlines new, British Airways, Easter Airways old and its current Eastern Airways striking blue and white scheme. It was captured here at Ronaldsway in its early days wearing the then British Midland blue and grey colours. (Jon Wornham)

Transall C-160F, callsign '61-ZW' of Esc 61 French Air Force registered F157 (c/n 157), at Ronaldsway on 31st May 1994. The aircraft was providing navigational training and had landed for fuel, both for the aircraft and crew! The airport had already got severe parking problems with a stranded MD83 taking up space when this large Transall arrived with little warning. (Philip Pain)

Hawker Siddeley HS-125-2 Dominie T1's XS733 (c/n 25059) and XS737 (c/n 25076) of 6 Flying Training School, based at RAF Finningley, visited the Island on 10th June 1994. These aircraft are used to train RAF Navigators, and the Island was a fairly regular lunch-stop for their training flights. However, these two conspired to arrange some training to co-incide with the annual TT races! *(Philip Pain)*

Junkers Ju 52/3m marked as D-AQUI but with the correct small registration, D-CDLH (c/n 130714) under tailplane, during a Lufthansa commemorative tour of the British Isles. It arrived from Dublin on 24th September 1994 and as part of the visit, Robert Edwin Clague DSM of Douglas was shown the aircraft and presented with a souvenir model of it. He had last flown in a Ju52 in 1943, a South African Air Force example from Cape Town to Egypt, a priority crew transfer of a Royal Navy ship's engineer. This visit to Ronaldsway was probably the first by a Ju52 since 1947, when a BEA machine (G-AHBP) made seven newspaper flights to the Island. *(Philip Pain)*

BAe ATP G-MANF (c/n 2040) of Manx Airlines, formerly G-LOGA of Loganair, seen at Ronaldsway on 3rd October 1994, following the fleet-swap between the two airlines. The aircraft is still in full Loganair livery, just the titling and registration have been changed. *(Philip Pain)*

P133 French Navy Lynx HAS.4 of 34F, 625 (c/n 119), captured during a refuelling stop en route to Northern Ireland on 25th October 1994. Strong westerly winds often resulted in military helicopters of all types running out of puff on their way to Northern Ireland and this is believed to be the only ever visit by a French military Lynx. *(Philip Pain)*

P134 An immaculate Wessex HCC.4 XV733 (c/n 733) of the Queen's Flight, based at RAF Benson. The aircraft was refuelling while on a ferry or positioning flight from Northern Ireland on 7th November 1994 and being flown by a 72 Squadron crew. It is the only known visit by a Queen's Flight Wessex to the Island. *(Philip Pain)*

Knight Air operated services between the Island and Leeds/Bradford airport using Embraer E110 Banderantie aircraft. Their G-OEAA (c/n 110256) was captured taxiing out towards the runway on its return flight to Yorkshire. The type were to have a relatively long stay at Ronaldsway, being used later by Comed Aviation and Flykeen. One example of this type is preserved at the local aviation museum. (Jon Wornham)

At the end of their passenger service career, many machines see further use as a cargo aircraft. This is the case with this Handley Page Dart Herald G-STVN (c/n 188) that began life with Swiss based Globe Air in May 1965, later operated in France before being converted to cargo configuration and joining the Channel Express fleet, then known as Express Air Services in 1978. It was withdrawn from use in 1997. (Jon Wornham)

Wittman W.8 Tailwind G-BOHV (c/n 031-11151) at Andreas Airfield on 29th April 1995, with Beagle Pup G-AVZP (c/n 121-008) behind. The occasion was a 'fly-in', thus increasing the number of light aircraft seen at this otherwise quiet airfield. The wartime control tower is to the rear left. (Philip Pain)

Two Jetstream T.2 observer trainers XX481 (c/n 251) and XX483 (c/n 264) of 750 Squadron, Fleet Air Arm, from RNAS Culdrose. The pair are seen on 9th June 1995 when they came visiting for the TT, and were hosted by Manx Airlines Engineering. *(Philip Pain)*

A type that is now commonplace at Ronaldsway is the Let 410. However, this visit by UR 67199 (c/n 790305) of Air Ukraine, on 1st September 1995 was believed to be the very first visit by a Let 410, and by Air Ukraine. The aircraft was on a sports parachuting tour, and came to the Island to explore the market here. On introduction to the then Airport Director, who also took the picture, the crew stood to attention! *(Philip Pain)*

Bell 214 OY-HCS (c/n 31150) of Greenlandair in Iceland called in for fuel on its delivery flight, on 12th June 1996. This remains the only known visit by this airline that operated a wide variety of types. *(Philip Pain)*

Shorts SD360s had a long career serving Ronaldsway both in passenger and freight configuration. Here BAC Express SD360 G-TMRO (c/n 3712) is seen parked up at Ronaldsway between cargo flights. The aircraft is named 'City of Newcastle' and had started life with Jersey European Airways, now Flybe. *(Author's Collection)*

Fouga CM-170 Magister IAC 215 (c/n 3656) of the Irish Air Corps, taken on 15th September 1997. There were five Magisters present, all just one week away from retirement from service. They had (most unusually) flown from Dublin to RAF Leuchars in Scotland for the annual Battle of Britain air display, where they performed as a team. They had planned to return direct to Dublin, but thankfully fuel reserves ran short, and with very little notice they diverted into Ronaldsway, making the one and only visit of the type. *(Philip Pain)*

Manx Airlines liveried BAe ATP G-MANC (c/n 2054) is seen with its engines running and about to move off stand, taxi out to the runway and get airborne. The aircraft is in the older Manx livery and later became the first of the ATPs to receive the new livery. *(Author's Collection)*

An official picture of the three Manx Airlines ATPs lined up at Ronaldsway. The 'odd man out' G-MANB (c/n 2055) is nearest the camera with G-MANC (c/n 2054) and G-MANA (c/n 2056) furthest away. The three are being prepared for their next flights, with a wide selection of airport and airline ground support vehicles visible. *(Author's Collection)*

When the Red Arrows display team are visiting the island to perform, one of the Hawk aircraft usually lands at Ronaldsway. However, on this occasion all ten of the aircraft landed and with the precision we have come to accept as normal for the Red Arrows, lined up on the tarmac, making this impressive view possible.

(David Ashworth)

British World Airlines sometimes provided stand-in aircraft to Manx Airlines in particular as they have the same type. British Aerospace ATP G-OBWP (c/n 2051) is seen on the old stand 7 at Ronaldsway with passengers boarding prior to departure. The aircraft was last noted as being in store at Coventry, presumably for possible future use with West Atlantic. *(Jon Wornham)*

An aircraft now transferred to the Philippines is this Gestair 1124 Westwind EC-GSL (c/n 353). It visited the Island in late September 2000 and is seen passing beneath the control tower. *(Jon Wornham)*

Bombardier built Dash 8s in their various forms have had a long association with Ronaldsway and now form the backbone of all services to London, Liverpool and Manchester. First introduced to Island services by Jersey European, now Flybe, they have also been used by British Airways and EuroManx. This example, a DHC8/Q300 G-JEDD (c/n 533), will have operated into Ronaldsway for Jersey European and was later OE-HBC in the EuroManx fleet spending several years based on the Island.

(Author's Collection)

British Aerospace intended to replace their successful 146, later RJ production with the RJX. Sadly only two flying examples were actually finished before the project was abandoned. Flybe had signed a deal with BAe for a number of the type and so they would have been visitors to the Island. However, this is about as close as the type actually got to landing on the Island when BAe RJX-85 prototype, G-ORJX (c/n E2376) made a low pass over Ronaldsway.

(Jon Wornham)

British Airways has its own flying club based at Wycombe Air Park in Buckinghamshire. The aircraft are painted in BA colours and are some of the smallest to wear the livery. Piper PA28-161 G-BNCR (c/n 28-8016111) visited the Island in July 2001 and was parked on the west apron. It carries the BA world livery with Chelsea Rose tail. *(Jon Wornham)*

During the summer of 2001 the Island hosted the Island Games, resulting in some interesting aircraft bringing competing teams to the Island. Scandinavian provided this McDonnell Douglas DC9/41 SE-DDT (c/n 47779/898) as flight SK7029 from Copenhagen, arriving at 11.50 on Saturday 7th July 2001. This was the last DC9/40 series aircraft build and has sadly now been scrapped. *(Barry Edwards)*

The Royal Flight fleet includes this HS125/700 ZE395 (c/n 257205), shown here in the flight's distinctive markings. It is parked on the old stand 4 during an official visit to the Island in October 2001. *(Jon Wornham)*

The revised Manx Airlines livery looked well on the ATPs as demonstrated by this fine view of G-MANA (c/n 2056) about to take off from runway 26 at Ronaldsway. The aircraft has since been converted to cargo use and flies for West Air Europe as SE-KXP. *(David Ashworth)*

The position of the Island in the middle of the Irish Sea means that it sees a fair amount of traffic 'calling in', often for fuel. Such was the case with this Cessna 406 G-TURF (c/n 0020) operating for the Coastguard. No doubt the crew will also take advantage of the brief stop to refresh themselves with a cup of coffee from the airport cafeteria. *(Jon Wornham)*

This RAF Wessex HC2 XR511 (c/n WA136) is seen with the buildings of King William's College in the background. It was visiting the college to take groups of the College's Combined Cadet Force for experience flights around Castletown Bay. This helicopter is now preserved in New Zealand. *(David Ashworth)*

A rareish visitor to the Island was this Irish Air Force Airtech CN235 MPA Persuader with fleet number 252 (c/n 85). It was conveying the Irish Prime Minister to a meeting on the Island and is seen being marshalled onto stand zero at Ronaldsway by the airport fire service.

(Jon Wornham)

Ronaldsway regularly saw the Embraer 145 jets in service with British Regional Airlines and later Flybe but, the smaller sister Embraer 135 has only made the occasional visit. Making an appearance in May 2003 was this French registered Embraer 135 F-GYPE (c/n 145492) in full Savoie livery. It was captured by the camera while parked on the old stand 1 at Ronaldsway, now stand 3.

(Jon Wornham)

Dragon Helicopters Jetranger, G-HPAD (c/n 1997), was employed on TT pleasure flights during the 2003 festival. The flights operated from a field adjacent to the Cooil Road on the southern outskirts of Douglas.

(Jon Wornham)

The many thousands of aviation passengers who spend hours straining to look out of tiny windows would welcome the view from this splendid looking Super Aero 45. Built by Strojirny Prvni Petilesky in 1956 the aircraft carries registration G-APRR (c/n 04-014) and was visiting Jurby airfield when it was captured by the camera. *(Jon Wornham)*

Locally owned Aerospatiale AS350B helicopter G-OMCC (c/n 1836) is seen while on a visit to the Creg-ny-Baa Hotel on the famous TT course. Powered by a single Turbomeca Arriel 1b engine the aircraft was built in 1985. In the distance can be seen Douglas Bay and the Carnane radio transmitter station. *(Jon Wornham)*

Jurby Airfield in the north of the Island has the central mountains as a backdrop. During the 2003 air show at the field, this General Electric Co J-47-Ge13 powered North American Aviation Inc built F86A Sabre 48-8178 FU-178 (G-SABR c/n 151-083) has just landed and is about to taxi off the runway. *(Jon Wornham)*

Parked outside hangar 292 at Jurby is this Supermarine 509 Spitfire T9, PT462 also registered as G-CTIX (c/n 151-43547). Sadly this hangar is no longer suitable for aircraft storage as one of the doors has been welded shut. It has recently been used to store a number of buses that have now moved across the airfield to the new transport museum but, is still home to a Leopard Moth. *(Jon Wornham)*

Manx Flyers Aero Club used this Cessna 172H for a few years in the early 2000s. Registered G-CCCC (c/n 175-55822) it is seen here on approach to Ronaldsway airport with another pilot under instruction. The aircraft has since moved away from the Island and is now registered G-RVRI. *(Jon Wornham)*

This Bombardier Dash8/Q200 G-JEDX (c/n 541) was later in the EuroManx fleet as OE-HBB and was based at Ronaldsway. It is seen here on 27th August 2003 while visiting during British European, now Flybe, days while operating their Belfast City to London City via Ronaldsway service. The Q200s have the same engines as the larger Q300s and so offer a spirited performance. *(Barry Edwards)*

Emerald Airways had a fleet of Hawker Siddeley HS748s, many in the livery of their previous owner with the fleet names painted out. Here G-SOEI (c/n 1689) is captured at Ronaldsway on 27th August 2003 during its day stop having arrived with the morning post from Liverpool. A couple of the former Emerald aircraft now fly in the Janes Aviation fleet. *(Barry Edwards)*

A relatively recent recruit to the Woodgate Aviation fleet is this American Champion Aircraft Corporation, Champion 8KCAB G-IGLZ (c/n 914-2003). Delivered new to an operator in Wickford Essex, it arrived on the Island in late 2003 when only a few months old. *(Jon Wornham)*

The relatively quiet runway at Ronaldsway allows the airfield to be used for training, in particular practice approaches, take-offs and landings. The RAF make good use of this and on this occasion the crew landed and went off to explore the Island leaving the aircraft available for its portrait to be taken. XX209 (c/n 144/312134) in all over black livery is on the west apron on 7th February 2004. *(Barry Edwards)*

The Island's geographical situation in the middle of the Irish Sea makes it a very useful stopping point for re-fuelling for aircraft involved in any maritime searches. The RAF's Rescue Sea King helicopter often calls in during routine training around the area. ZE369 (c/n WA948) is seen awaiting its fuel on the west apron with an Eastern Airways Jetstream 41 behind. *(Barry Edwards)*

On a bright sunny day in June 1968, Viscount 701 G-ALWF (c/n 005) gets airborne from Ronaldsway. The pilot will be concentrating on the aircraft's climb rate and has already retracted the undercarriage and the main wheels have almost stowed away, while the front one is already safely retracted and the protecting flaps closed. Take-off is about the busiest part of a flight for its crew. *(Stan Basnett)*

A splendid October 1962 picture of Fokker F27 EI-AKG (c/n 10119) in the livery of Aer Lingus, subtitled Irish International Airlines. It is interesting to note that the control tower sits alone on the airfield, unlike today when it is surrounded by terminal building and is indeed under threat, with a new tower now in operation. The Captain appears to be looking for something while bags are loaded into the hold and the steps are ready for the passengers. *(Stan Basnett)*

McAlpine Aviation Piaggio P166B G-ASPC (c/n 412) stands outside the terminal building in February 1970, long before any of the recent additions or indeed the now old wooden pier was added. This type is unusual in that the propellers are behind the wings rather than in the usual position in front. *(Stan Basnett)*

Who needs tarmac? Looking as if they have landed in a field these two Rollason Aircraft and Engines Ltd, Druine D31s are at Jurby airfield in May 1965. Nearest the camera is G-ASAM (c/n PFA595) and behind is G-ASDB (c/n PFA1600). The 3 and 4 on the tails would indicate that the machines were taking part in some form of competition based around the former RAF airfield. *(Stan Basnett)*

The main runway at Ronaldsway was strengthened during 1970 to allow heavier aircraft to lane. This super, late 1970 view, shows an early unidentified Boeing 737 in the white with green stripe livery of Air Lingus Irish International, on approach. The pilot has lowered the landing gear and extended the flaps and will be preparing to apply the brakes as soon as the aircraft has all its wheels safely on the runway. *(Stan Basnett)*

Aerobatics over Jurby. Displaying at the annual Jurby Air Show on 16th August 1981, are Woodgate Aviations' Piper Aztec G-CALL (c/n 27-7754061) and Navajo Chieftain G-CITY (c/n 31-7852136), the upper aircraft, make a fine sight in the skies over the airfield. *(David Ashworth)*

A South West Aviation DC3 and Cambrian BAC1-11 show off their different styles on the apron at Ronaldsway in June 1971. *(Stan Basnett)*

There are many aircraft and types that have had long associations with the Isle of Man but, Piper Navajo Chieftain G-CITY (c/n 31-7852136), must hold the record for the longest serving passenger aircraft based on the Island. It joined the fleet of City Air Links on 1st November 1978 and is still in regular use by the current owners, Woodgate Aviation. It is also the smallest aircraft painted into the livery and used in passenger service by Manx Airlines. It is seen here hiding behind one of the two F27s. *(David Ashworth)*

The first Comet civil jet aircraft came off the production line in July 1949, the modern day military Nimrod is still a direct descendant of that first machine. Here we have Nimrod MR2P 801 XV240 (c/n 8015) during a display at Jurby air show with its armoury doors open. These spectacular aircraft still visit the Island on training flights and can often be seen climbing away from the main runway at Ronaldsway after a practice approach. *(Stan Basnett)*

Ronaldsway as it used to be. Manx Airlines Viscount 816 G-BFZL (c/n 435) and BAC 1-11 G-WLAD (c/n 112) pose together on the west apron during May 1987. Note that the steps employed at the side of the aircraft are titled Isle of Man Airports Board, as is the Leyland truck in the foreground. *(Stan Basnett)*

DH.82A Tiger Moth, accurately restored in its wartime markings as DE208, G-AGYU (c/n 85265). Based at Ronaldsway for a few years it was captured by the camera on 17th July 1990, with former Airport Director, Philip Pain, in the cockpit. Phil notes that his actual flight in this aircraft was on a very cold November day! Because of its tailskid configuration, a grass runway strip was created especially for it, just to the south of runway 08/26 (probably still 09/27 then), with Ronaldsway becoming a four-runway airport again for a few years. *(Philip Pain Collection)*

Hawker Siddley HS748 Series I belonging to Janes Aviation, later Emerald Airways, G-BEJE (c/n 1556) in the colours of Skynet, one of their contract customers, at Ronaldsway on 4th December 1992. It was being used on Janes' daily general freight run, and was not the 'mail plane'. *(Philip Pain)*

An unusual visitor to Ronaldsway on 10th August 1993 was this De Havilland Aircraft Company DH114 Sea Heron built in 1956 and registered G-AORG (c/n 14101). Known as the 'Airfix' Heron it was rescued by a group of enthusiasts in Jersey after seeing military service and fully restored to flying condition. It had arrived with the Lieutenant Governors of Jersey and Guernsey for a meeting on the Island. *(Philip Pain)*

Easyjet Airbus A319-111 G-EZDX (c/n 3754) just before touchdown on runway 26 at Ronaldsway in June 2010. This new service from Liverpool started in late May, once again producing competition on the Liverpool route, a situation that has arisen several times in recent years and in each case has ended in tears. (Martin Nelson)

G-EZDX

Netherlands registered Schreiner North Sea Helicopters Sikorsky S-61N MkII, PH-NZG (c/n 61753) makes a rare sight during a stop at Ronaldsway. The helicopters were generally used to ferry crew to and from the many rigs in the North Sea. Schreiner Aviation Group was purchased by the CHC Helicopter Corporation in 2005. *(Jon Wornham)*

P-51D Mustang "Old Crow" N167F (c/n 44-73877) made a rare appearance on the Island, for the VJ day anniversary display along Douglas promenade and was photographed at Ronaldsway on 7th May 1995. The aircraft wore authentic wartime markings of the 357th Fighter Group, based in England, and flown by 17.25 Kills Ace, Bud Anderson. *(Philip Pain)*

Bolkow Bo 209 Monsun 150FF, G-AZDD (c/n 143), at Jurby on 12th July 1996. This was the (then) annual air display and Schneider Cup air races at Jurby, with many light aircraft in the background, and the wartime control tower to the left. *(Philip Pain)*

The Royal Flight aircraft are based at Northolt Aerodrome in West London and are used to convey members of the Royal Family on official journeys. BAe146/100 CC2 (c/n E1021) is seen at Ronaldsway. It is parked on the old stand 8, now 12, where it is under the watchful eye of a guard situated in the security box for the overnight stop. *(Barry Edwards)*

This Antonov biplane was a rare sight at Ronaldsway. It is an AN2R Colt with registration LY-MHC (c/n 1G215-33) and called in for fuel. It was captured as it passed beneath the control tower before the airport layout was changed and this area became parking stands. (Jon Wornham)

Looking more like a paint colour chart than a helicopter, this Hughes Tool Co 369HS G-SOOC (c/n 11103545) came to Ronaldsway in July 2000. Powered by a single Allison 250-C18A powerplant, it posed for the camera while parked on the east apron with the now demolished hangar 1 visible behind. (Jon Wornham)

Over the years the Island has had several 'celebrity' aircraft, one such being British Aerospace 146/200 G-MIMA (c/n E2079). This aircraft joined the Manx Airlines fleet in March 1993 at which point it wore the older Manx livery. It received the new Manx livery in October 1998 and later the British Airways Chatham livery. It is seen here in its BA livery at Ronaldsway stranded due to heavy overnight snow. *(Barry Edwards)*

British Regional Airlines were one of the first to order the new Embraer 145 aircraft from the Brazilian manufacturer. By the year 2000, 15 aircraft had been delivered to the Island and Embraer offered British Regional the 300th aircraft off the production line. Photographed minutes after arriving on stand zero at Ronaldsway on 27th August 2000 is G-EMBP (c/n 145300), complete with clever 300th markings on the side of the fuselage, incorporating the British Regional logo. *(Barry Edwards)*

One of the biggest aircraft types to have visited the Island is the Airbus A321. On 8th May 2005 My Travel provided their A321/211 OY-VKD (c/n 1960) for an early morning charter. With its wings extending beyond the stand markings the impressive looking aircraft, is seen here on the old stand 4 at Ronaldsway.
(Barry Edwards)

Brand new Royal Flight Keystone Helicopter Corporation Sikorsky S-76c G-XXEB (c/n 760753) over the Island on 29th September 2009, the day after it was officially added to the UK aircraft register. It was manufactured and delivered with its American registration N753V. *(Jon Wornham)*

Palmair have made several visits to the Island in recent years, on this occasion with a charter from Bournemouth Hurn airport. Boeing 737-5H6 G-PJPJ (c/n 27355) rests on the west apron while its passengers enjoy various sightseeing trips around the Island. Visible in the background is J31 G-OAKI (c/n 718). (*Martin Nelson*)

Heavy showers to the west of Ronaldsway provided this super rainbow over Aero Charter Antonov AN26, UR-DWB (c/n 6207) parked on the old stand 1. The aircraft had arrived with the morning post and would spend the day on the Island before taking the evening outgoing post to Liverpool. (*Jon Wornham*)

An unidentified British Aerospace Harrier Jet is seen during preparations for a flying display at Jurby airfield. These remarkable machines that are now nearly 40 years old, are still among the most versatile military aircraft ever built with their vertical take-off facility. (*David Ashworth*)

RAF Avro Vulcan XM605 (c/n 698) visited the skies over the Island again in September 1985, this time at Ronaldsway. The wonderful shape of these fine machines is clearly evident. (*Stan Basnett*)

Shortly after taking over Manx Airlines, British Airways replaced the ATPs with Dash8/Q300s from the Brymon Airways fleet. The very last ATP departure from Ronaldsway was the BA4409 to Manchester on Saturday 28th March 2004. The aircraft G-MANH (c/n 2017) is 'powering back', a practice now rarely seen, from the old stand 6 under guidance from ground crews. *(Barry Edwards)*

Long before Manx Airlines was taken over by British Airways, it had up to 11 ATPs in British Airways livery for use on its franchised routes. Several received the short lived BA world livery with varying tail colours. One of these was G-MAUD (c/n 2002), registered in the name of a long serving employee of the company, and is seen here at Ronaldsway with the terminal building and South Barrule in the background. *(Barry Edwards)*

ATR 72s now operate daily into Ronaldsway but when this example arrived on 6th April 2004, they were considered an unusual visitor. On this occasion Channel Islands-based Aurigny provided their G-BWDB (c/n 449) for a charter service. The picture was taken at 05.55 the following morning with the aircraft parked on the old 'stand zero' and the lights of the terminal building behind. *(Barry Edwards)*

Some early passenger flights to the Island were operated by De Havilland Aircraft Co Ltd DH89A Rapide aircraft. G-AKIF (c/n 6838) seen here at Duxford Air Museum in Essex, was used by the original Manx Airlines between October 1947 and September 1958. The aircraft is still in flying condition and makes regular pleasure flights from its base in South East England. *(Barry Edwards)*

Thought to be the first time an Aruba registered aircraft had visited Ronaldsway, this Eurocopter EC135 T1, P4-XTC (c/n 0115) arrived in July 2004 and was parked on the grass adjacent to a couple of the older buildings on the airfield. Helicopters have the significant advantage that they do not need a runway, nor a hard standing on which to park, allowing considerable choice of parking place. *(Jon Wornham)*

Woodgate Aviation operate a fleet of smaller aircraft but, had this Jetstream 3102 G-CCPW (c/n 785) in their fleet for a while. Seen here parked on a damp west apron at Ronaldsway on 17th January 2005, the aircraft is now operated by Highland Airways. *(Barry Edwards)*

Making a rare appearance at Ronaldsway on 27th August 2003 was this Irish Air Force Aerospatiale SA-365F Dauphin 2 helicopter 245 (c/n 6168). It is on the old stand zero on the west apron awaiting refuelling and departure back to its home base. *(Barry Edwards)*

Another unusual visitor to the Island, also dropping in for refuelling while on route from France to Canada was this Conair Convair 640 fire fighting aircraft. Registered C-FKFA (c/n 100) its bulging water tank, that holds 7,950 litres is clearly visible under the fuselage. *(Jon Wornham)*

Before settling down with its own liveried fleet of aircraft, EuroManx used a wide variety of aircraft, from an equally wide range of operators, on their routes. Club 328 was associated with the airline and on at least one occasion their executive configured Dornier 328 jet OE-HAA (c/n 3200) was used on commercial flights. The aircraft is seen here at Ronaldsway on 1st February 2005 during a private charter visit to the Island. *(Barry Edwards)*

EuroManx chartered a couple of ATR42s from Farnair while waiting for their own fleet to arrive. HB-AFD (c/n 121) is seen parked on the old stand 5 at Ronaldsway, on 2nd April 2005, awaiting its next rostered flight. The aircraft is still in the Farnair fleet. *(Barry Edwards)*

During the 2005 UK General Election campaign, the Liberal Democrats chartered Atlantic's ATR42 G-IONA (c/n 017). This aircraft was at the time a regular on EuroManx routes and on a couple of weekends turned up at Ronaldsway in full election livery to operate EuroManx services. It is seen here at Ronaldsway on a dull damp 16th April 2005. *(Barry Edwards)*

The Hawker Siddeley, later BAe, family have long been associated with Ronaldsway, the small Jetstream 31 being no exception. Eastern Airways used this example, G-OAKJ (c/n 795), on their daily service between the Island and Leeds/Bradford. It is seen here about to depart from the Island for Yorkshire on 1st July 2005. An Aer Arann ATR42 is visible behind. *(Barry Edwards)*

Russian built Mil Mi8T helicopter HA-HAS (c/n 7970) visited Ronaldsway in July 2005 while actually taking part in filming at Jurby airfield. *(Jon Wornham)*

An RAF Chinook makes a spectacular sight during a display at the Jurby Air show in August 2005. What the pilot didn't do with that machine is not worth mentioning! *(Barry Edwards)*

71

Jurby airfield in the north of the Island has been host to a number of air events in recent years, with large numbers of visiting aircraft attending. Preserved Hawker Sea Hawk WV908 (c/n 6123), dating from 1954, is receiving attention before giving a short display over the airfield. (*Barry Edwards*)

Wing walkers are always an attraction and again were a regular at Jurby. Boeing PT17 Kaydet A75N1 N74189 (c/n 75-717) is seen parked on the apron areas during a break in activity on 7th August 2005. Sadly these events have now ceased and there seems little prospect of them being re-instated in the foreseeable future. (*Barry Edwards*)

Another type that has seen long service operating to and from the Island is the Dakota. In recent years Air Atlantique have operated a charter flight from Coventry to coincide with the annual TT and Manx Grand Prix festivals, the aircraft spending the day at Ronaldsway, allowing plenty of times for photography! G-AMRA (c/n 15290/26735) was the rostered aircraft on 29th August 2005 and was captured resting on the old stand 9. *(Barry Edwards)*

The registration of this aircraft very much matches its looks! Short Brothers Skyvan3/100 G-PIGY (c/n SH1943) made a rare appearance at Ronaldsway in March 2006 and parked adjacent to the Manx Flyers flying club. The aircraft was previously registered LX-JUL, it was first operated by the Mauritanian Air Force and is now used as a parachute training aircraft. *(Jon Wornham)*

During the weeks following the demise of Emerald Airways these Antonov AN26s became regular visitors to the Island with the daily post flight. YL-RAB (c/n 7310508) was the rostered aircraft on 10th May 2006. The impressive buildings of King William's College are clearly visible in this view. (*Barry Edwards*)

Following the collapse of Emerald Airways, EuroManx needed a higher capacity aircraft to operate on the Liverpool route. The answer came from Coventry based Atlantic who had this ATR72 G-HERM, originally registered for operation in the Channel Islands, available. It is captured during push back from stand at Ronaldsway before taxiing and departure to Merseyside on 13th May 2006. (*Barry Edwards*)

The presence of the local flying club provides a good selection of locally owned and visiting private aircraft. Creeping in between the inbound evening commercial flights is this Yakovlev Yak18T HA-YAJ (c/n 0133), on finals to runway 26. Despite the relatively late evening of 27th May 2006, there was sufficient light available for the camera to nearly stop the propeller. *(Barry Edwards)*

Dash8/Q200 OE-HBB (c/n 541) of EuroManx is on final approach to runway 26 at Ronaldsway with an evening arrival on 27th May 2006. The captain had extended the flaps, lowered the landing gear and will have received his 'Cleared to Land' instruction from the control tower. Once on the ground he will receive further instruction as to his taxi route to his allotted parking stand. *(Barry Edwards)*

Eastern Airways acquired the entire fleet of BAe Jetstream 41s from British Regional when it was taken over by British Airways. Eastern were quick to repaint the fleet into their own livery, that has since changed. In the earlier livery of Eastern Airways, G-MAJC (c/n 41005) gets airborne from Ronaldsway with the evening flight to Birmingham on 2nd June 2006. The company have since ceased operating to the Island. *(Barry Edwards)*

The presence of the local flying club ensures a good variety of smaller aircraft using the airfield at Ronaldsway. Here we have Cessna 421C G-MUVG (c/n 421C-1064) during its take-off climb from runway 26. The aircrafts wheels can be seen already stowed away, just inside the two engines. *(Barry Edwards)*

Following the withdrawal of 146/200 G-MIMA, British Airways allocated BAe 146/100 G-MABR (c/n 1015) to the Island for operation of the London routes. In full Chatham livery the 146 is seen here getting airborne from runway 26, with the evening BA4327 service to London Gatwick on 2nd June 2006. The wheels are still part way through the stowing process and will no doubt still be rotating at this point. *(Barry Edwards)*

After a period of wide variety of types on regular services, the takeover of BA Connect by Flybe and the demise of EuroManx have meant that a large number of flights into and out of Ronaldsway are handled by Dash 8/Q400s. Here we have Flybe DHC8/402 G-JEDR (c/n 4087) captured shortly after landing on runway 26 at Ronaldsway and about to turn off the runway and make its way 'to stand'. *(Barry Edwards)*

Eastern Airways operate a number of Saab 2000 aircraft. This example, G-CDKA (c/n 2000/006), displaying a special livery, arrived with a charter flight on 17th June 2006. The livery depicts the skyline of Aberdeen but, the aircraft has since been repainted into Eastern's standard livery. *(Barry Edwards)*

Blackpool based Comed Aviation operated the Blackpool and Belfast routes for a number of years, using E110 Banderantie aircraft and a selection of Piper Aircraft Corporation types. This Aztec G-TAXI (c/n 27-7305085) carries an apt registration and is captured by the camera during an extended stop over at Ronaldsway. *(Barry Edwards)*

British Airways introduced Bombardier Dash 8/Q300s to the Manchester route, replacing the ATPs. Having arrived with the last flight of the day, G-NVSA (c/n 451) is parked on stand 4 at Ronaldsway. The aircraft will have been cleaned and had a number of engineering checks before being closed up and secured for the night. The late evening sun of 25th June 2006 lights the side of the aircraft. *(Barry Edwards)*

During the early months of 2006 a new airline announced it was setting up on the Island and would operate flights to Blackpool, Belfast City and Belfast International (Aldergrove) airports. The aircraft type would be the Czechoslovakian built Let Kunovice L410. In the week before the first flight, a demonstration flight for members of the local travel industry operated to Belfast. Shortly before departure the L410, HA-YFG (c/n 861813) is seen on the new stand 11 at Ronaldsway on 13th July 2006. *(Barry Edwards)*

Andreas airfield is located in the north of the Island and is now privately owned. It is used by many local enthusiasts to house their aircraft and is no doubt cheaper than Ronaldsway. Locally owned Piper PA32/300 G-AVFU (c/n 32-40182) was captured at the airfield on 16th January 2007. *(Barry Edwards)*

Another aircraft at Andreas on the same day was this Piper PA28 G-BTAM (c/n 28-90093). While providing aircraft parking facilities in the north of the Island, there is very limited hangar accommodation. *(Barry Edwards)*

Emerald Airways held the Isle of Man post contract for many years and also operated up to two other daily cargo flights into the Island. Most of these flights were operated by their fleet of HS748s but this SD360 did appear on a few occasions. Painted in what was the 'new' Emerald colours it is registered G-JEMX (c/n 3715) and was one of only a few aircraft to receive this livery. *(Author's Collection)*

Fairchild Metroliner EC-ITP (c/n B6-789B) operating for Manx2.com climbs away from runway 08 at Ronaldsway with a flight to Belfast. This type has become a regular sight on the Island, although disappeared during the recent winter. *(Barry Edwards)*

Another type that was once a fairly rare visitor to the Island is the ATR family. EuroManx were first to base the type on the Island and Aer Arann now have one ATR72 night stopping and operate the twice daily service to London City, as well as twice daily trips from Dublin. Aer Arann's first ATR72 EI-REA (c/n 441) heads back to Dublin with an afternoon service. *(Barry Edwards)*

Ronaldsway is also home to the Ashley Gardner Flying School who operate this Piper Corporation PA28/140, G-AYPV (c/n 28-7125039) seen here on finals to runway 08 on 23rd March 2007. *(Barry Edwards)*

Eastern Airways painted their Jetstream 41 G-MAJM (c/n 41096) into this special livery to promote north east England. It is captured by the camera as it prepares to turn and line up on runway 08 at Ronaldsway with the afternoon service to Newcastle. The aircraft was delivered new to British Regional Airlines in British Airways livery in late October 1996. *(Barry Edwards)*

There are large numbers of aircraft owned by residents of the Isle of Man, many now on the Manx register, and this is one example. Registered G-LEKT (c/n 1181) it is an Avions Pierre Robin, CEA DR400/180, powered by a single Lycoming O-360-A3A engine and is unusual in that its wheels do not retract in flight. *(Barry Edwards)*

Helicopters are used all over the world for air ambulance duties, due mainly to the agility and ability to land almost anywhere. The Isle of Man is no exception and although there is no permanent aircraft, helicopters are provided during the annual TT race festival and Manx Grand Prix fortnight. Taken during the centenary TT festival of 2007, G-SKYW (c/n 5261) is an Aerospatiale AS355F1 machine and is seen occupying one of the two helipads at Nobles Hospital. *(Barry Edwards)*

As well as helicopters, fixed wing aircraft are also used for ambulance flights. Visiting the Island during the 2007 TT festival was this German registered Dornier 328 jet D-BADC (c/n 3216), its all over yellow livery making it hard to miss! Quite what the broom was for remains a mystery. (*Barry Edwards*)

Helicopter pleasure flights are sometimes operated as part of the TT festival, taking off from a field on the outskirts of Douglas. During the 2007 races, Bell 206 helicopter G-LIMO (c/n 45476) was used for the flights. It is seen here while between flights and parked just of the Cooil Road in Douglas. (*Barry Edwards*)

The airport fire station with its watch tower and the Langness peninsular provide a backdrop for Atlantic Airlines ATP G-OAAF (c/n 2029) as it taxies out to runway 26, on its return flight to East Midlands, having arrived earlier in the day with the Island's post. *(Barry Edwards)*

The centenary TT festival of 2007 attracted thousands of visitors to the Island and many of the airlines responded well with increased capacity. Acquired by British Regional Airlines for their Gatwick to Inverness service, this 146/300 G-OINV (c/n 3171) was borrowed to operate the London services from the Island. With a full complement of 112 passengers the aircraft is seen getting airborne from Ronaldsway with the first trip of the day to London on Saturday 9th June 2007. *(Barry Edwards)*

Pilatus Britten-Norman Ltd BN2B-26 Islander, G-BUBJ (c/n 2267), is captured outside the former Manx Airlines Hangar on a visit to the Island in June 2007. Built on the Isle of Wight these tiny aircraft are ideally suited to routes serving small islands and many are operated within the Scottish Islands. This machine is now one of them having transferred to Hebridean Air Services Ltd and been re-registered G-HEBS. *(Jon Wornham)*

When British Airways CitiExpress was formed it included the former Brymon Airways and its fleet of aircraft, all eventually finding their way into the Flybe fleet. Here we see former Brymon Embraer 145 G-ERJA (c/n 145229) on stand 3 at Ronaldsway in early July 2007. It was one of the few 145s to receive a full Flybe livery. *(Barry Edwards)*

Manx Airlines would have been 25 years old in 2007 but had already been absorbed into British Airways. Needless to say, little persuasion was needed to organise a party to mark the anniversary. Held at Mount Murray, this mock-up ATP doorway was constructed over the entrance to the bar. The bar was also temporarily re-named Scruph's Bar in memory of the late Captain Winston Oliver. *(Barry Edwards)*

The Island's situation in the middle of the Irish Sea makes it an ideal landing point for over-flying aircraft that have developed a fault that requires an 'as soon as possible' landing. This was the case on 3rd August 2008 when Embraer 195 G-FBEH (c/n 19000128) landed with smoke in the cabin. After attendance from the Ronaldsway fire service the aircraft was towed to stand 2, to await further attention by Flybe engineers. *(Jon Wornham)*

West Air Europe ATP SE-KXP (c/n 2056) taxies in towards the main hangars at Ronaldsway for maintenance at the airline's facility. This was a trip home for this aircraft as it had previously seen service with Manx Airlines as G-MANA. (Jon Wornham)

French Air Force Twin Otter 730/CA (c/n 730) taxies towards the apron at Ronaldsway after arriving from France on 15th April 2009. (Jon Wornham)

Built in Germany by Extra Flugzeugproduktions-Und Vertriebs Gmbh Extra Ea 300/L G-ZEXL (c/n 1225) and G-ZXCL (c/n 1223) together on the apron at Ronaldsway. (Jon Wornham)

In April 2007 the Isle of Man started its own aircraft register and series of registrations prefixed with the letter M. The first two Manx registered aircraft were M-ELON and M-BWFC and were unveiled at a small ceremony at Ronaldsway on 1st May 2007. A couple of years later on 13th July 2009, Cessna Aircraft Company 525B (CJ3) M-ELON (c/n 525B-0148) taxies up to its hangar after landing. (Jon Wornham)

Sikorsky S76 G-URSA (c/n 760699) has taxied into Area Victor adjacent to the Aviation Museum, its engine stopped and shutdown checks in progress. Previously registered N2582J it was only just a year old when this picture was taken on 24th July 2009. *(Jon Wornham)*

Another early addition to the Manx register was this locally owned Sikorsky Aircraft Corporation S-76B M-ERRY (c/n 760356). It was previously G-BWDO and originally on the Manx register as M-ONTY. *(Jon Wornham)*

Local operator Manx2.com uses a number of Dornier 228 aircraft on its routes in and out of Ronaldsway. Here D-IFLM (c/n 8046) is lined up on runway 26 and preparing for take-off on 29th September 2009. *(Jon Wornham)*

Locally owned Cirrus Design Corporation SR20 GTS M-YGTS (c/n 1972) joined the register on 28th August 2008 and is seen here at Ronaldsway on 23rd October 2009. It has since transferred to the UK register. *(Jon Wornham)*

Embraer–Empresa Brasileira de Aeronautica S.A. EMB-500 M-KELY (c/n 50000040) in all over grey livery is captured arriving at Ronaldsway on a wet day in November 2009. *(Jon Wornham)*

Royal Air Force Bombardier BD-700-1A10 Sentinel R1 'Snapshot one' ZJ690 (c/n 9107) passing overhead on a practice approach on 10th December 2009. *(Jon Wornham)*

The 1962 built Cessna Aircraft Company Cessna 185A Skywagon G-BXRH (c/n 185-0413) looks immaculate and certainly does not give away its age, tucked away out of the weather at Ronaldsway.

(Jon Wornham)

United States Army C12U Argus12 84-0173 (c/n BL103) taxies for departure to Hahn, after making a rare visit to Ronaldsway on 10th February 2010. *(Jon Wornham)*

During 2009 Aer Arran entered into an agreement with Aer Lingus to operate some of their internal flights as Aer Lingus Regional. This meant some Aer Arran aircraft being painted into Aer Lingus green livery. One such machine, ATR 72 EI-REM (c/n 760), is seen at Ronaldsway on 20th March 2010. *(Jon Wornham)*

An event that attracted extensive publicity throughout the Island was the appearance of this RAF C17A ZZ175 (c/n F185/UK-5). The aircraft made several practice approaches and provided some spectacular aerobatics during its stay. It is seen here commencing a climb after a low approach and go round on 13th July 2010. *(Jon Wornham)*

One man and his flying machine. Brightly coloured Quik GT450 Microlight G-CEGT (c/n 8208) passes over Marine Drive, Douglas on 15th August 2010. Even machines like this have to pass stringent safety tests and be properly registered before they are allowed to take to the skies. (Jon Wornham)

Causing a stir over the south of the Island is this RAF Tristar K1 ZD949 (c/n 193V-1159) as it climbs away after a practice approach on runway 26 on 21st September 2010. (Jon Wornham)

Local tour operators have for many years arranged 'direct flights' to various destinations, usually within Europe. Air Malta are one such operator who provide a number of direct flights each year. Here their Airbus A320 9H-AEJ (c/n 2186) is seen occupying stand 4 at Ronaldsway before departing with a full load of passengers on 7th June 2006. King William's College and Langness can be seen in the background. *(Barry Edwards)*

Front Cover: Manx Airlines took delivery of their second British Aerospace ATP on 22nd March 1989. Registered G-OATP (c/n 2005) it is seen here during an air-to-air publicity photography session with Port St Mary and the Calf of Man in the background. The aircraft was re-registered G-MANM in October 1994 and remained in the fleet after the takeover by British Airways. The aircraft now flies for West Atlantic as SE-MAM. *Author's Collection*

Back Cover Far Left: Excitement surrounded the arrival of Eurocypria Airbus A320/231 5B-DBB (c/n 256) at Ronaldsway on 7th February 1993. Weighing in at 74 tonnes it was, at the time, the heaviest aircraft to land at the airport and the first visit of the type. It was operating a direct charter flight to Cyprus. *Philip Pain*

Back Cover Left: One of the first visits of an Airbus A319 was made by this German registered machine D-APAB (c/n 1955) of PrivatAir on 30th August 2003. It was captured by the camera preparing for departure with the wing of resident 146/200 G MIMA providing a cover for the photographer. *Barry Edwards*

Back Cover Right: Shortly after taking over Manx Airlines, British Airways CitiExpress replaced the ATPs with Dash 8/300s from the former Brymon Airways fleet. BACX was later re-branded BA Connect but only a few aircraft received the new branding before the whole operation was sold to Flybe. One example that did receive the new branding was the DHC8/Q311B, G-BRYY (c/n 519). It is seen here on finals to runway 08 at Ronaldsway with a service from Manchester on 23rd March 2007. *Barry Edwar*

Back Cover Far Right: The Manx Airlines' Shorts SD360s carried a number of variations of the livery. Here we se SD360/100 G-BKMX (c/n 3608) lined up and ready for take-off from runway 26 at Ronaldsway displaying a single d with two lighter green lines along the fuselage. It was removed from the UK register on 20th May 2009 and transferred to America. *Author's Collec.*